AF752347

The Right Hon. Lord Millett was appointed Queen's Counsel in 1973. He served as a Judge of the High Court of Justice 1986–94, a Lord Justice of Appeal 1994–98 and a Lord of Appeal in Ordinary 1998–2004. He continues to sit on the Court of Final Appeal of Hong Kong, having been appointed in 2000. Lord Millett has published numerous influential articles on equity and commercial law, including, as Queen's Counsel, 'The Quistclose Trust: Who Can Enforce it?' (1985) 101 *LQR* 269 and his very influential article on *Lister v. Stubbs* (1890) 45 Ch D 1, 'Tracing the Proceeds of Fraud' (1991) 107 *LQR* 71, which was heavily relied upon by the Privy Council in departing from that decision in *Attorney General for Hong Kong v. Reid* [1994] 1 AC 324. Other major contributions include 'Restitution and Constructive Trusts', published in a book of essays in honour of Professor Gareth Jones, Cornish et al. (eds), *Restitution Past, Present & Future* (Hart Publishing, 1998). Lord Millett is widely considered to be the leading equity judge of his generation in England.

THE **MCPHERSON LECTURE** SERIES

On Villainy

Peter Millett

VOLUME ONE

UQP

First published 2007 by University of Queensland Press
PO Box 6042, St Lucia, Queensland 4067 Australia

www.uqp.uq.edu.au

© The Right Hon. Lord Millett of St Marylebone 2007

This book is copyright. Except for private study, research, criticism or reviews, as permitted under the Copyright Act, no part of this book may be reproduced, stored in a retrieval system, or transmitted in any form or by any means without prior written permission. Enquiries should be made to the publisher.

Typeset in 12.5/16.5pt Bembo by Post Pre-press Group, Brisbane
Printed in Australia by McPherson's Printing Group

Produced with the assistance of the TC Beirne School of Law at the University of Queensland.

Cataloguing-in-Publication Data
National Library of Australia

Lord Millett of St Marylebone.
The McPherson Lecture Series Vol. 1: On Villainy

Bibliography.
Includes index.
ISBN 978 0 7022 3590 0.

I. Identity theft. 2. Fraud. I. Title.

364.163

CONTENTS

PREFACE

In 2005 the TC Beirne School of Law at the University of Queensland decided to establish a new annual lecture series. The series was to be named in honour of one of Queensland's and Australia's finest judges, the Hon. Mr Justice Bruce McPherson of the Queensland Court of Appeal. That decision was particularly fitting given the judge's association with the school, as both a member of the teaching faculty early on in his career and as a PhD graduate of the school. The school was delighted when Lord Peter Millett accepted its invitation to give the first series of lectures, and these were delivered in March 2006. It was also fitting that the inaugural lectures be delivered in 2006, since this was Mr Justice McPherson's last year of service on the bench.

We thank Lord and Lady Millett for the time and energy they devoted to travelling to Brisbane, particularly in light of the fact that Lord Millett had broken his leg shortly before the trip and endured much discomfort to see through his initial commitment. The Milletts' visit was an enormous success, helped considerably by the warm welcome they received from the Governor of Queensland, the Hon. Quentin Bryce, the Chief Justice of Queensland, the Hon. Paul de Jersey, and the judges of both the Supreme Court of Queensland and the Federal Court of Australia, and members of the local profession (with a special mention of the partners of Minter Ellison who hosted the Milletts at a dinner during their visit).

Lord Millett's lectures were held in the Banco Court at the Supreme Court of Queensland, for the use of which we acknowledge the Chief Justice's generous support. The lectures were very enthusiastically received, and it is my considerable pleasure and honour to present them for a wider audience in this book. The school is also particularly grateful to Ms Madonna Duffy and her team at the University of Queensland Press for the positive and energetic way in which they embraced the launch of the McPherson Lectures as a series under the Press's imprint. I believe this book to be a most fitting start to the series, which I hope will produce stimulating scholarship of interest and lasting importance throughout the common law world, and indeed beyond.

Charles Rickett
Sir Gerard Brennan Professor of Law and Head
TC Beirne School of Law
University of Queensland

TABLE OF CASES

VILLAINY IN VENICE

CHAPTER ONE

VILLAINY IN VENICE

My subject in this lecture is the trial scene in *The Merchant of Venice*. I want to look at it as a lawyer and a judge, not as an actor, a Shakespearean producer or a Shakespearean scholar, for I am none of those things. I was moved to prepare this paper by a program on English television in which David Suchet and Patrick Stewart, two English Shakespearean actors, discussed playing the part of Shylock. To my astonishment, neither mentioned the trial scene at all. Yet this is surely the pivotal scene. It helps to resolve the main problem that the play poses: is Shylock a villain or a victim; or both villain and victim? It may also help to resolve a subsidiary question: did Shylock always intend to exact his pound of flesh? Or did he change his mind later, and if so when?

The trial scene is the most famous and certainly the best-written trial scene in the theatre. Portia's cross-examination of Shylock is a superb example of the art. All students of advocacy should study it and note the skilful way in which she cross-examines Shylock. She never descends into the arena or argues with Shylock in the manner of a bad trial lawyer in an American film. She keeps her distance and remains aloof. She remains fully in control throughout, the better to manipulate Shylock. She sets out to win his confidence, while carefully getting him to close off all avenues of escape before springing the trap shut.

Yet a careful reading of the text yields a darker tale. For Portia is not an advocate. She has no business to be cross-examining Shylock at all. She is not, as the audience might assume, counsel for Antonio. She is the judge; and far from seeking to give a just and impartial verdict, she deliberately sets out to ruin Shylock and makes fraudulent use of the justice system to achieve her purpose.[1]

It is convenient to begin the narrative with Count

---

1 Since the trial takes place in Venice, a civil law jurisdiction, it may be suggested that Portia is an examining magistrate. The trouble with this is that Portia's questioning is not inquisitorial but adversarial. It is a great mistake to equate adversarial questioning with hostile questioning. The point is that Portia is not engaged on an impartial quest for the truth, but on eliciting damaging answers that will prevent Shylock from defending himself when Portia turns the tables.

Bassanio, even though he is not the first member of the cast in order of appearance. He is a scoundrel and a wastrel. Having run through his fortune by being (in his own words) 'something too prodigal',[2] he tells his friend, the merchant Antonio, who is also his biggest creditor, that he has a scheme which will enable him to 'get clear of all the debts I owe'.[3] He says that he is laying suit to a gentlewoman, one Portia, who lives in Belmont, and whom he describes to his friend as 'a lady richly left'.[4] Not only is she possessed of a fortune, but she has no father or guardian to protect her. She is, he adds, also fair and virtuous. But these desirable qualities seem to be something of a bonus; they are of secondary importance to Bassanio. What matters to him is her money. She is a prize, not a lover. Indeed, the whole play is about money, not love. Everyone's motivation is mercenary.

To woo his lady successfully, however, Bassanio needs to put on a show of wealth, and he lacks the means to buy the necessary finery. He asks Antonio to lend him still more money, admitting that the debt he already owes him is lost; but he has the effrontery to

---

2 Act I, Scene I.

3 ibid.

4 ibid.

say that a further loan should see all his debts repaid. It is clear to both these self-styled gentlemen that Portia's fortune is the only source from which Bassanio can ever hope to repay Antonio.

Antonio is willing to oblige Bassanio. There has been much speculation as to the reason why Antonio should accommodate his friend. It has been suggested that he is gay and that Bassanio is his lover. There is no evidence to support this beyond Antonio's opening line, 'I know not why I am so sad',[5] and his farewell to Bassanio in the trial scene when he expects to die:[6]

> Commend me to your honourable wife:
> Tell her the process of Antonio's end;
> Say how I loved you, speak me fair in death . . .

This seems poor evidence of a very 21st-century analysis. Moreover, if Bassanio is Antonio's lover, why should he help him to woo his maid? I think that the explanation of Antonio's conduct is much simpler. He sees it as a way of getting his money back. As usual, his motive is entirely mercenary.

Although Antonio is willing to oblige his friend,

---

5 ibid.

6 Act IV, Scene I.

he is not in a position to do so. He has no ready money, since, as he tells Bassanio, his fortunes 'are at sea'[7] and he has 'neither ... money nor commodity to raise a present sum'.[8] But he tells Bassanio to try and raise the money elsewhere and he, Antonio, will stand surety for the debt.

Bassanio then applies to the Jew Shylock for a loan of 3,000 ducats for three months on the security of Antonio's bond. Three months is a dangerously short period within which to offer repayment, seeing that he has no hope of doing so until he marries Portia and gets his hands on her money. Moreover, Antonio's bond is a surprising security to offer Shylock. Shylock believes Antonio to be good for the money, though he certainly does not regard him as a good man in any other sense. Nor *is* he. He is a rabid anti-semite who is in the habit of publicly insulting Shylock whenever he meets him in the Rialto, calling him to his face a misbeliever and a dog, and even spitting on his coat. When Shylock asks him why, in such circumstances, he can expect any favours from him,[9] Antonio tells him that he is not prepared

---

7 Act I, Scene I.

8 ibid.

9 'Hath a dog money? Is it possible
A cur can lend three thousand ducats?' (Act I, Scene III).

to change his ways, but will continue to call him dog and spit upon him. He arrogantly demands that Shylock should indulge him as an enemy, not as a friend.

Antonio despises Shylock because he lends money at interest, a practice which Antonio considers to be usury and contemptible in a gentleman. This is rank hypocrisy. Antonio is in trade himself. He is in the import and export business. He carries on his business for gain, and openly boasts about the large profits he hopes to make. Yet he demands that Shylock should do what he is not prepared to do himself and put his money at risk without hope of gain.

Shylock for his part has nothing but contempt for Antonio. He says that he hates him because he is a Christian, but more because he foolishly lends out money without interest, thereby bringing down the rate of interest in Venice. This is certainly part of the story; money is a mainspring of the play. But it is surely not the whole story. Shylock is a serious man, unlike the other characters, who are fops and lightweights. His hatred has a deeper foundation. He is proud of his tribe and ancient lineage; and he hates Antonio for the contempt he shows for his 'sacred nation'.[10] Antonio has:

---

[10] Act I, Scene III.

> disgraced me and hindered me half a million, laughed at my losses, mocked at my gains, scorned my nation, thwarted my bargains, cooled my friends, heated my enemies, and what's his reason? I am a Jew.[11]

He does not hate Antonio simply for what he has done; he hates him for his anti-semitism.

Shylock sees an opportunity to get even with Antonio or, as he puts it, to 'catch him once upon the hip'.[12] He will have his revenge. As Shylock is later to observe, the desire for revenge is a peculiarly Christian trait:[13]

> . . . [I]f you wrong us, shall we not revenge? If we are like you in the rest, we will resemble you in that. If a Jew wrong a Christian, what is his humility? Revenge. If a Christian wrong a Jew, what should his sufferance be by Christian example? Why, revenge. The villainy you teach me I will execute, and it shall go hard but I will better the instruction.

So Shylock agrees to accommodate Bassanio, and even to forgo any interest on the loan. But he tells

---

11 Act III, Scene I.
12 Act I, Scene III.
13 Act III, Scene I.

Antonio that he needs some earnest of repayment on the due date, and demands a pound of Antonio's flesh as security. Three points are to be observed about this extraordinary condition. First, Shylock describes it to Antonio as 'a merry sport'.[14] Second, the pound of flesh is to be 'an equal pound',[15] that is, one pound precisely. Third, it is to be cut off and taken from whatever part of Antonio's body pleases Shylock.

Antonio rashly agrees to the condition, being supremely confident that his ship will come home a month before the day stipulated for repayment, and that he will be able to repay the debt well within the time agreed. The parties duly attend on a notary to execute what Shylock again describes to Antonio as 'this merry bond'.[16] Shylock, who does not himself have 3,000 ducats in ready money, borrows the sum from Tubal, a fellow Jew, and lends it on to Bassanio, who promptly spends it on finery in which to woo Portia.

Bassanio's suit succeeds, and he and Portia are duly married. Unhappily, the three months' period of the loan has by now expired, and Bassanio has not made repayment. Shylock calls on Antonio to honour

---

[14] Act I, Scene III.

[15] ibid.

[16] ibid.

his bond, but Antonio's confidence in his ability to repay the debt was misplaced. Shylock, for his part, is distraught, for his beloved daughter Jessica has just eloped with one Lorenzo (a Christian and a man of levity whom Shylock despises), aided, as Shylock believes, by Bassanio and his friends. Moreover, they have taken 4,000 ducats (rather more than Bassanio has borrowed) and some jewellery which they have stolen from him.

Not surprisingly, Shylock is not in a forgiving mood. He demands his pound of flesh, and makes it clear that he will not accept late payment from Antonio or anyone else. In this he undoubtedly goes too far. But Antonio is a hypocrite who boasts of his own moral stature while deriding that of others. It is understandable that Shylock should insist that such a man be held to his word; and he must surely be forgiven much, given the state he is in at the loss of his daughter. It is after learning of her betrayal of her father, her people and her faith that Shylock tells Tubal to fetch an officer to arrest Antonio as a prelude to legal action.

David Suchet argues that this is the moment when Shylock finally makes up his mind to exact his pound of flesh. I agree with Suchet that Shylock did not intend to do so at the outset. His object was to humiliate

Antonio. To obtain a public judgment against him and then generously refrain from enforcing it would be the greatest humiliation – more than Antonio could bear; it would put him in Shylock's debt for ever. But it does not follow that having Antonio arrested shows that Shylock had changed his mind. To obtain a judgment meant holding a trial, and this meant having Antonio arrested. It is entirely possible that even now Shylock did not intend to enforce a judgment, though a judgment he must have. I like to think that he was provoked by Portia into changing his mind during the trial.

Whatever the truth, Shylock sues Antonio for his pound of flesh, and the case comes on for hearing before the Duke. The Duke presides over the trial, but he does not adjudicate. He sends for Bellario, a learned doctor, 'to determine' the case.[17] These words make it clear that Bellario is summoned to act as judge, not as counsel for Antonio. Bellario, however, does not come. Portia, Bassanio's wife, posing as one Balthasar and masquerading as a Doctor of Laws, comes in his stead, bearing a letter which she has forged herself and which purports to come from

---

[17] Act IV, Scene I. This procedure was common in Italy at the time.

Bellario and commends the young man's learning in somewhat over-fulsome terms.

Portia falsely tells the Duke that she has come from Bellario. She then proceeds to determine the case. There is no doubt that she acts as judge. She makes all the relevant rulings. She gives judgment in Shylock's favour on his claim to a pound of Antonio's flesh. And when she has succeeded in turning the trial into a criminal one, she pronounces Shylock guilty of a capital offence and indicates the nature of the mandatory sentence which (she says) the law imposes. The only order that the Duke makes is to commute the death penalty and substitute a fine for a confiscation order. In doing so, the Duke exercises his executive function as head of state, not a judicial function as judge in the cause.[18]

The parties themselves address Portia as the judge. As the case sways back and forth, each in turn compliments her on her judicial sagacity. Thus Shylock says: [19]

> A Daniel come to judgment! Yea, a Daniel!
> O wise young judge, how I do honour thee!

---

18 Acting in relation to the sentence in a criminal matter. The Duke gives no ruling of any kind in relation to Antonio's civil liability, which is what the case is supposed to be about.

19 Act IV, Scene I. The reference is to Daniel, the young judge in the apocryphal story of Susannah and the Elders.

Later he had exclaimed of Portia: 'O wise and upright judge!', 'Most rightful judge!' and 'Most learned judge!'[20] And when the tables are turned, Gratiano, one of Antonio's supporters, sarcastically echoes Shylock's words: 'O upright judge! Mark, Jew. O learned Judge!' and 'O learned judge! Mark, Jew. A learned judge!'[21] and addresses her as a second Daniel:[22]

> A Daniel still say I, a second Daniel!
> I thank thee, Jew, for teaching me that word.

At the outset of the trial Portia is asked by the Duke if she is acquainted with the facts of the case,[23] and she confirms that she is. She then asks: 'Which is the merchant here? And which the Jew?'[24]

As one Shakespearean scholar[25] has observed, Portia's inability to distinguish between Antonio and Shylock surely indicates that Shylock should not be played, as he too often has been, as a grotesque stage Jew. Both in dress and appearance he ought to be indistinguishable from his

---

[20] ibid.
[21] ibid.
[22] ibid.
[23] ibid. 'Has your Lordship had an opportunity to read the papers?'
[24] ibid.
[25] Michael Taylor, *The New Penguin Shakespeare*, Penguin, London, 1995, p. 63.

tormentors except by age and seriousness of purpose. The only alternative is to surround Shylock with his Jewish friends, all similarly garbed, so that Portia is not seeking to distinguish between Antonio and Shylock but between the two contestants and their respective supporters.[26]

As the judge, Portia proceeds to conduct the trial in a most extraordinary fashion. Antonio has several obvious lines of defence to Shylock's claim, some of them cast-iron, yet she either fails to consider them at all or questions Shylock in a manner which is deliberately designed to get him to close them off:

1. Shylock had described the condition to Antonio as 'a merry sport'.[27] From his asides, we know that inwardly he meant it seriously, but at the time he had intimated to Antonio that he did not. It is clearly arguable that, so far as Antonio is concerned, it was a jest not intended to create

---

[26] This is how the scene is played in the recent Pacino film; all the Jews were made to wear red hats to distinguish them from Christians. But it is an artificial reading of the text. Portia asks a single question in two parts, not two separate questions. Moreover, Shylock's friends would not have attended the trial. They would have made themselves scarce, fearing retribution from Antonio's friends whatever the outcome. And if they had been present, Shakespeare would have given them something to say: he usually lets his extras mutter their sentiments, like a Greek chorus, perhaps in order to draw the groundlings into the action. He would have put the words 'Oh wise young judge' into their mouths.

[27] Act I, Scene III.

a legal obligation. Moreover, that is how it would have been understood objectively by reasonable people. Salarno, for example, assumes that Shylock will not enforce the bond. He tells Shylock: 'Why, I am sure, if he forfeit, thou wilt not take his flesh: what's that good for?'[28]

Shylock replies: '[I]f it will feed nothing else, it will feed my revenge.'[29] But this is after the event. Private reservations, not disclosed at the time, cannot affect the true nature of the bargain.

Portia never considers this defence and never puts it to Shylock. She merely asks Antonio if he admits the bond. When he does, she intimates that in that case Shylock's claim must succeed: 'Then must the Jew be merciful',[30] that is, give up a good claim.

2. The condition is manifestly contrary to public policy and illegal or *contra bonos mores*, and Portia knows this perfectly well, for she later cites the relevant statute. But she never considers it as a ground for dismissing Shylock's suit, as it plainly is.

---

28 Act III, Scene I.

29 ibid.

30 Act IV, Scene I.

3. The condition is a penalty and so unenforceable. She never considers this, even though Shylock several times describes it as 'the penalty and forfeit'[31] of his bond.
4. The condition is merely a security for a debt. As such, it is not enforceable if the debt is paid, even if payment is tendered after the due date. Portia must have known this, for the historic dispute between equity (represented by Lord Ellesmere LC) and law (by Sir Edward Coke) was recent and much publicised when the play was written, though it was not finally settled in Lord Ellesmere's favour for another fifteen years.[32] Yet when her husband, Bassanio, tenders the money (which he must have obtained from her), Portia falsely rules that it would be contrary to precedent for Shylock to accept it.

Why, then, does Portia not simply dismiss Shylock's claim when Antonio obviously has a complete defence?

---

31 ibid.

32 By the commission established by James I following the great case of *Glanvill v. Courtney* (1615) Cro Jac 343.

It is because she is after bigger game. She does not want Shylock's suit dismissed, leaving her husband's debt outstanding. She is bent on obtaining Shylock's money. She is plotting to defraud him, which she proceeds to do very effectively.

First, as we have seen, she lulls Shylock into a false sense of security by indicating that, unless he is merciful, he must gain the suit. Hypocritically, she waxes eloquent on the subject of mercy, a quality which she has no intention of showing towards Shylock when her turn comes. In this she is not attempting to persuade Shylock but to provoke him. She tells Shylock:[33] 'Then *must* the Jew be merciful.' To which Shylock is provoked into replying: 'On what compulsion *must* I, tell me that.'[34]

Portia's great speech on mercy makes it impossible for Shylock to be merciful. This would be Portia's victory, not his. It is a commonplace that aggressive cross-examination tends to strengthen the witness's evidence and make him more obdurate. It is usually a novice's mistake; but here it serves Portia's purpose. From this moment, at least, Shylock must exact his pound of flesh.

---

33 Act IV, Scene I.

34 ibid.

I have spoken this much
To mitigate the justice of thy plea,
Which if thou follow, this strict court of Venice
Must needs give sentence 'gainst the merchant there.[35]

Mercy here is standing in for equity. But Shylock stands for law. His response,

I crave the law,
The penalty and forfeit of my bond,[36]

precludes Shylock (as Portia intends) from invoking equitable principles in his own defence when she turns the tables on him.

Shakespearean scholars agree that the trial scene represents the perennial conflict between law or strict justice on the one hand and equity on the other. This is so; but it would be a gross oversimplification to hold Shylock as standing for law and Portia for equity. She invokes equity only when it suits her, and in order to obtain Shylock's response to use against him later.

In the same vein she forbids Bassanio to offer to discharge the debt. When Bassanio implores her to:

---

35 ibid.
36 ibid.

> Wrest once the law to your authority,
> To do a great right, do a little wrong,[37]

a clear invocation of equity, she falsely tells him that

> there is no power in Venice
> Can alter a decree established. [38]

When, relying on her, Shylock declines to withdraw the claim which she has told him must succeed, and rejects a tender of thrice his money, Portia gives judgment and formally awards Shylock a pound of Antonio's flesh: [39]

> The court awards it, and the law doth give it.[40] ('The court' is Portia, who is again identified as the judge.)

But Portia, who actually holds the bond in her hands, has deliberately misread it. She pretends that it refers to a pound of flesh nearest Antonio's heart. It does not. It authorises Shylock to take the pound of flesh from such

---

[37] ibid.

[38] ibid.

[39] ibid.

[40] Hood Phillips observed: 'We might as well say that a person entitled to an easement may not leave footmarks on the land because this was not expressly mentioned in the grant': see O Hood Phillips, *Shakespeare and the Lawyers*, Methuen, London, 1972, p. 93.

part of Antonio's body as it might please him. Portia's fraudulent reading now leads her to advance the most extraordinary proposition that, because the bond does not mention blood, Shylock must take the flesh without shedding a jot of Antonio's blood. Even the most literal methods of construction, which give undue primacy to the words used and abjure the more modern, purposive construction, do not compel so ridiculous a meaning to be placed on the condition in the bond. It is obviously impossible to take a pound of flesh without spilling blood; and accordingly leave to spill blood is necessarily to be implied. It is a general maxim of the law, cognisable in every civilised country, that the grant of a right (the pound of flesh) assumes the conditions (the spilling of blood) that make the exercise of the right possible.

Portia knows perfectly well that the bond entitles Shylock to spill any necessary blood. But she has already foreclosed Shylock's reliance on any implied term to that effect. She has asked him to have a surgeon available to stop Antonio's wounds, 'lest he do bleed to death'.[41] This was a clever ploy on her part, which succeeded when Shylock responded as expected: 'Is it so nominated in the bond?' Portia admitted that it was

---

41 Act IV, Scene I.

not. 'But what of that?'[42] she asked. 'I cannot find it; 'tis not in the bond,' Shylock had replied.[43]

After this exchange Shylock cannot ask for any words to be implied into the bond, however much legal principle and common sense may require it. He may have his pound of flesh according to the tenor of the bond, but must shed no blood in the taking of it. Furthermore, he must take neither more *nor less* than an exact pound, not even if the difference should be no more than the estimation of a hair (a forensic exaggeration that defies the universal maxim of the law *de minimis non curat lex*). This last condition, scarcely less absurd than the former, is also not the law. It would be a trespass for Shylock to take more than the pound to which he is entitled, but he would commit no wrong by taking less.

Having been thus hoodwinked, Shylock now abandons his claim to the pound of flesh and tries to settle the case. He asks for 9,000 ducats. Bassanio offers to pay this sum, presumably intending to use Portia's money. But Portia is having none of it. She rules that Shylock shall have 'nothing but the penalty'.[44] This is plainly wrong. Why should not the parties settle the case on

---

42 ibid.
43 ibid.
44 ibid.

terms to which all three of them agree? Shylock now reduces his demand to the 3,000 ducats he is owed. Portia rules that he is not even entitled to this.

> Thou shalt have nothing but the forfeiture.[45]

This too is not the law, but a travesty of the law. True it is, as Portia reminds everyone, that Shylock has previously refused such an offer in open court; but that cannot prevent him from changing his mind. There is no estoppel; Bassanio has not acted to his detriment. He still owes 3,000 ducats. In any case, Shylock is entitled to release Antonio as surety without releasing the principal debtor Bassanio. But then, unknown to Shylock, the judge has a financial interest in ruling that her husband's offer, which he is making at her expense, must be rejected.

Portia finally turns the tables on Shylock completely. She accuses him of having made an unsuccessful attempt on Antonio's life contrary to a statute of Venice. This is ludicrous. Shylock has merely instituted legal proceedings. Had his case succeeded, and had Antonio died as a result, it would have been

---

45 ibid.

justifiable homicide; his death would have been occasioned by an order of the Court (indeed of Portia herself), and could not be attributed to any wrongful act on the part of Shylock. It would have been otherwise if Shylock had sought to deceive the Court into giving a false verdict; but he had not.

Portia now rules that Shylock's life is at the mercy of the Duke and that all his goods are forfeit, one half to the state and the other to Antonio. Needless to say, these are criminal penalties, and Portia has no right to pronounce such a sentence in civil proceedings in which Shylock is not even the defendant but the plaintiff.

The Duke, exercising the executive power of clemency, now commutes the death sentence, and indicates that, if Shylock humbles himself, he may be persuaded to discharge the confiscation order and substitute a fine. This dismays Portia, who sees the object of her scheme slipping away. She protests that the Duke may discharge that part of the order which is for the benefit of the state, but not that part which is for Antonio's benefit. Knowing Antonio's generosity of spirit when disposing of other people's property, she probably assumes that Antonio will pass anything he receives to her husband, Bassanio.

Instead, however, Antonio asks the Duke to remit

all penalties provided that Shylock assign one-half of his estate to Antonio to be held in trust upon Shylock's death for Lorenzo, the man who stole his daughter. And for this 'favour' Shylock is required to execute an immediate deed of gift of all he possesses to Lorenzo and his daughter; and to become a Christian. Under overwhelming pressure, believing Portia to be an impartial and independent judge who has rendered an honest judgment in accordance with law, and in order to escape the confiscation of all his worldly goods, Shylock submits to the order and undertakes to execute a deed of gift in appropriate terms.[46]

It is sometimes suggested that Shylock gets off lightly, but that is impossible to accept. Spared his life, he has to beg to be allowed to keep the means whereby he lives; he is stripped of everything that makes his life worth living: his child, his friends, his faith, his self-respect, and even his identity, for he defines himself by his faith. Shylock's 'I am content'[47] are words of utter desolation. As for the others, Jessica keeps the money and jewellery she has stolen and her husband gets the reversion to Shylock's estate on his death. Bassanio gets

---

[46] The gift is testamentary in character, and unknown to the parties Shylock's deed is ineffective to create a valid gift in law.

[47] Act IV, Scene I.

to keep the money he has borrowed without having to repay it. And Antonio enjoys the sweetest revenge of all by forcing Shylock to convert to Christianity, a step which Shylock will have regarded as sacrilegious and which will cost him the society of all his friends. History does not disclose whether he feels obliged to repay Tubal, the friend from whom he borrowed the money to lend to Antonio; but as a man of the most punctilious probity he probably does.

The play is usually classified as a comedy,[48] which means that we are expected to believe that everyone (or everyone except Shylock) will live happily ever after. But Shakespeare hints that they will not. Jessica finds that, far from being welcomed as a convert to Christianity, she is regarded as a pork-eating Jew for whom there is no mercy in heaven. She begins to doubt Lorenzo's love, telling him that he was guilty of 'stealing her soul[49] with many vows of faith, and ne'er a true one'.[50] Bassanio, who has been guilty of some foolishness over a ring that Portia has given him, swears that he will never again break faith with her.

---

48 It has usually been so regarded. But as early as 1709 Nicholas Rowan said that he could not but think that it was designed by the author as a tragedy. Heine, too, counted the play among Shakespeare's tragedies.

49 Act V, Scene I. Her soul, not her heart. She begins to see that she has given more than her love.

50 Act V, Scene I.

And Antonio, who reminds Bassanio that he once lent his body for his wealth (and who has evidently learned nothing from the experience), rashly dares to become his surety again with his 'soul upon the forfeit'.[51] We have learned enough of Bassanio's character to know that he will soon run through his wife's money and get into debt again; and that it will be only a matter of time before he breaks his promise to her and Antonio is once again called on to honour his word. But this time it will be his immortal soul that is at risk, and the cause will be determined justly and honestly and by a greater judge than Portia, for 'shall not the Judge of all the earth do Justice?'[52]

The question most frequently debated is whether Shylock is victim or villain, though in truth his character is far too complex to be classified as wholly one or the other. Productions of the play have oscillated between the malignant caricature of comedy and the dignified figure of tragedy. Hazlitt observed that 'Shakespeare's malignant has outlived Mr Cumberland's benevolent Jew'.[53] He described Shylock as '*a good hater*, "a man no less sinned against than sinning". If he carries his

---

51 ibid.

52 Genesis 18:25.

53 William Hazlitt, *Characters of Shakespeare's Plays*, JM Dent & Sons, London & Toronto, 1926, p. 206.

revenge too far, yet he has strong grounds for the "lodged hate he bears Antonio?"'[54]

The great Edmund Kean rescued Shylock from the previous caricature as 'a decrepit old man, bent with age and ugly with mental deformity, grinning with deadly malice, with the venom of his heart congealed in the expression of his countenance, sullen, morose, gloomy, inflexible, brooding over one idea, that of his revenge'.[55] This portrait, Hazlitt pointed out, derived from other actors, not from the play itself. Kean played Shylock as a tragic figure, as did Sir Henry Irving, who considered that Shakespeare intended to enlist the audience's sympathies on Shylock's side. The whole force of an 'old, untainted religious aristocracy',[56] he said, is made manifest in his person.

Heine saw a performance of the play at Drury Lane, when, he recorded, a beautiful pale-faced English woman stood behind him in the box and called out repeatedly, 'The poor man is wronged'. Heine himself did not spare Shylock's enemies. They were, he said,

---

54 ibid. (emphasis in original).

55 ibid., p. 211.

56 Michael Taylor, *The New Penguin Shakespeare*, Penguin, London, 1995, p. 48.

'hardly worthy of unlacing his shoes'. Antonio was 'a weakling and without energy'; Bassanio was 'a true fortune hunter who borrows money to buy fine clothes to entice a wife with a fat dowry'. The other Venetians were 'a sorry lot'. However much we must hate Shylock, we cannot blame him if he despises 'those people.'

Despite the complexity of his character, the trial scene identifies Shylock for any lawyer as a victim not a villain. The villain is Portia. She is cruel, relentless, cunning, deceitful and (despite her eloquence on the subject) merciless. It is obvious that her judgment cannot possibly stand. She is not an impartial and independent judge, but the wife of the principal debtor. That alone would be enough for any appellate court to set aside her judgment and order a new trial. But it goes much further than that. Portia's conduct is not merely partial but fraudulent. By recourse to forgery and false impersonation, by a deliberate misreading of the critical document and by her increasingly bizarre rulings she obtains the discharge of her husband's debt without payment and puts the disposal of Shylock's worldly goods at the order of her husband's biggest creditor and closest friend. The Court's decrees are not merely consequent upon the rulings of a judge who is *parti pris* to the cause. They are the machinery by which she practises a wicked fraud on her husband's creditor, the man without whose help her husband would not have gained her hand in marriage.

The play is not a simple comedy, for it has the darkness of injustice at its heart. Nor is it a simple tragedy, for Shylock's ruin is set among scenes of gaiety and light-hearted party-going. I regard it as a tragic-comedy, like *Romeo and Juliet*, which begins as a romantic comedy and ends as a tragedy. *The Merchant of Venice* is a tragedy set in the midst of a comedy of manners. Life is often like that. But how true to life is the play? Miss Prism's words come to mind:[57]

> The good ended happily, the bad unhappily. That is what fiction means.

But who are the good and who are the bad? If Antonio and his friends are 'the good' and Shylock is 'the bad', then 'the good' are worthless and contemptible and 'the bad' is the one serious character who deserves not only our pity but our respect. He is the only character with any moral stature. To play him as a stage Jew is to diminish one of Shakespeare's greatest and most complex creations.

---

[57] Oscar Wilde, *The Importance of Being Earnest*, Act II.

CIRCULAR TRANSACTIONS

CHAPTER TWO

CIRCULAR TRANSACTIONS

When appearing for the Inland Revenue in the English Court of Appeal, I once posed the question:[1] 'Can two penniless tramps sitting on a bench in the park lend each other £1 million? (One lends the other £1 million repayable on demand; the recipient promptly deposits the sum borrowed with the other on call.)' Templeman LJ, a Chancery judge who later became a Law Lord, replied: 'No; of course they can't.' Donaldson LJ, a Commercial judge who later became Master of the Rolls, replied: 'Yes; of course they can. That's banking.'

Is this a real transaction? We can surely agree on two

---

1 *Eilbeck v. Rawlings* [1980] 2 All ER 12.

things. First, it should not make any difference if the tramps exchange worthless cheques each of which is honoured on the faith of the simultaneous receipt of the reciprocal cheque drawn on the same bank. Or if a messenger from a clearing bank, escorted by a policeman, brings a banker's draft for £1 million, which is passed from hand to hand before being taken away again. If it is not a real transaction without the cheques or banker's draft, their presence does not make it a real one. Second, it should not matter how many persons there are in the circle. In the example given, there are only two, and the transaction appears to be completely artificial. It ought not to make a difference in principle if there are three, four or six persons in the circle, but the more persons there are the less artificial the transaction appears. And when large numbers of people are involved, most of whom are strangers to each other, and the transaction has not been prearranged, you have got banking.

But what if our two tramps are former property developers who have fallen on hard times and owe each other £1 million? Can they mutually repay each other? Surely the answer is yes. You do not need to have any money to release a debt. There is no difference between mutual repayment and mutual release. The two tramps do not need to exchange cheques. They can set the two debts off against each other; they need only write each other a letter. What if there are three persons in the circle? What if A owes $1 million to B who owes $1 million to C who in turn owes $1 million to A? There are several ways to discharge all three debts. It could be done by a circular series of assignments, or by a tripartite deed of mutual release. But the simplest way is simply to pass a cheque round the circle. So it is clear that the mere fact that the transaction is circular does not mean that it is not a real transaction having real effect.

We are led into a blind alley if we ask whether the money that is passed round the circle is 'real money', or whether the transaction is a 'real' transaction. These questions are meaningless. We should consider whether the transaction is honest or dishonest, and whether the circularity is of the essence of the transaction or merely incidental. We should examine each of the payments that make up the circle, identify the critical payment, and consider whether, in the circumstances in which it was made, it achieved its object.

The reported cases of circular transactions fall into two main categories: (1) schemes concerned with the provision or application of a company's share capital, and (2) tax avoidance schemes. The first category covers cases where men of straw seek to provide a company with the appearance of substantial share capital, or resort to the company's own funds in order to purchase its shares. The second covers cases in which taxpayers engage in artificial tax avoidance schemes in order to attract tax relief. Neither enterprise is meritorious, and both have aroused much judicial indignation. Indignation is a poor substitute for analysis. The cases are full of purple passages and references to 'sham', 'charade', 'pretence', 'contrivance', 'magic' and 'unreality', but little in the way of logical reasoning.

The most celebrated description of a circular transaction is to be found in the judgment of Templeman LJ in the leading English case concerned with an artificial tax avoidance scheme. In a graphic and memorable passage, he said that the case represented:[2]

> ... yet another circular game in which the taxpayer and a few hired performers act out a play; nothing happens save that the Houdini taxpayer appears to escape from the manacles of tax. The game is recognisable by four rules. First, the play is devised and scripted prior to performance. Secondly, *real money and real documents are circulated and exchanged.* Thirdly, the money is returned

---

2 *WT Ramsay Ltd v. Inland Revenue Commissioners* [1979] 1 WLR 974, 979 (emphasis added).

by the end of the performance. Fourthly, the financial position of the actors is the same at the end as it was at the beginning save that the taxpayer in the course of the performance pays the hired actors for their services. The object of the performance is to create the illusion that something has happened, that Hamlet has been killed and that Bottom did don an ass's head, so that tax advantages can be claimed as if something had happened. The audience are informed that the actors reserve the right to walk out in the middle of the performance, but in fact they are the creatures of the consultant who has sold and the taxpayer who has bought the play; the actors are never in a position to make a profit and there is no chance that they will go on strike. The critics are mistakenly informed that the play is based on a classic masterpiece called 'The Duke of Westminster' . . .

1 Provision of a company's share capital

The earliest reported case I have found involving a circular transaction is *Gray v. Lewis*.[3] The case concerned the flotation of a public company. The promoters wanted to provide it with a share capital

---

[3] (1873) 8 Ch App 1035.

of £200,000. They did not have £200,000, so they resorted to a circular money transaction. They agreed with the company's directors and the bank as follows: (1) the bank would discount the promoters' notes to the amount of £200,000; (2) the promoters would pay the £200,000 to the bank to the credit of the company's account in payment of £5 per share for 40,000 shares in the company to be allotted to members of the public who subscribed for them; (3) the £200,000 should remain frozen in the company's bank account until the notes became due; and (4) it should then be applied in payment of the notes. The bank credited the promoters' account with £200,000; the promoters paid the £200,000 into the company's account at the bank; and the bank gave a certificate to the Stock Exchange (without which the shares would not have been marketable) that the company had £200,000 in its bank account. The notes were dishonoured and the bank duly repaid itself out of the £200,000, leaving the company entirely without funds.

In due course the company was wound up, and the shareholders brought a derivative action on behalf of the company against the directors and the bank to recover the £200,000 as money paid out in breach of trust. The action was dismissed.

The Court of Appeal held: (1) that if the money in the

company's bank account belonged to the company, the action was misconceived; the proper remedy was a simple action in debt by the company to recover the money in its account; for the company's agreement that its money should be applied in payment of the notes was *ultra vires* and was therefore no answer to the company's demand to be paid the sum in its account; but (2) that in fact the £200,000 did not belong to the company at all, for the whole transaction was an illegal and fraudulent scheme out of which no rights could arise as between the parties to it, and accordingly the company suffered no loss.

James LJ said:[4]

> The whole thing was a trilateral contrivance . . . for the purpose of deceiving the committee of the *Stock Exchange* by making it appear that [the company] had moneys which they had not . . . Everybody connected with the transaction must have been fully aware that the whole thing was a sham from the beginning to the end, and from a sham no action or suit arises either at law or in equity.

But his Lordship did not explain why the transaction was a sham.

---

[4] ibid., 1053.

Mellish LJ was more explicit. He said:[5]

> [T]he transaction appears to me . . . to be an entire sham. There is, under the pretence of dealing with these large sums of money, no real advance to anybody. Nobody is put in funds. [The promoters] get no money which they can deal with; [the company] gets no money which they can deal with; the bank make no advance to anyone except for the mere nominal period during which it is paid out and taken back again. There is no real monetary transaction at all . . . it is quite obvious that nothing whatever had been advanced or paid over at all . . . It was a transaction on the face of it for the purpose of making it appear that 40,000 shares had been allotted and paid for, whereas, in reality, no shares had been allotted and paid for.

His Lordship did at least explain why the money never belonged to the company as its share capital:[6]

> The money paid in never was . . . the money of [the company]. *They never had the control over it; they never could draw cheques upon it . . .*

---

5 ibid., 1054.

6 ibid., 1055 (emhasis added).

He held that the legal effect of the transaction was that anyone who was deceived by the transaction (i.e. anyone who was induced to subscribe for the shares or to buy them believing them to have been honestly subscribed for and paid for) had his own personal remedy against the persons who had deceived him. But the transaction had no further effect. Since the money never belonged to the company, the directors were not guilty of a breach of trust in paying it to the bank.

I had a similar case in the 1960s while I was standing junior counsel to the Department of Trade and Industry. At the time there was a statutory requirement that an insurance company could not carry on insurance business in the United Kingdom unless it had a minimum paid-up share capital of £50,000. The promoters wanted to establish a company to carry on insurance business in the United Kingdom but had not got the necessary £50,000. So they incorporated their own bank in the Cayman Islands with a paid-up share capital of two cents, arranged for it to provide them with a banker's draft for £50,000, paid the £50,000 into an account in the company's name at a London bank in return for the issue of its shares, and immediately procured the company to deposit the £50,000 with their Cayman Islands bank in order to meet the banker's draft.

I was instructed to apply for the winding up of the company on the ground that it had provided financial assistance in connection with the original subscription for its own share capital. 'How could it possibly provide financial assistance to any one to do anything?' I asked. 'It hadn't any money.' I applied to wind the company up, not on the ground that it had provided financial assistance in connection with the subscription for its own shares, which was absurd, but on the ground that it had no share capital at all. I remember describing the Cayman Islands bank as 'literally a two bit company'.

In this case there was no underlying reality at all. The Cayman Islands bank did not have any money. Its draft for £50,000 was worthless. It was bound to be dishonoured as soon as the company presented it for payment but for the immediate deposit of £50,000. All the payments were interdependent. Each of them depended for payment on the corresponding receipt. The parties were pulling themselves up by their own bootstraps. In *Gray v. Lewis*, by contrast, the parties used real money. The bank had substantial resources. It paid real money into the company's bank account. But it was not willing to allow the money to be paid out except to itself. It remained in complete control of the money throughout. Yet the conclusion in both cases was the same; the company had no share capital. This shows that the result does not depend on whether the parties used 'real' money. Mellish LJ gave the reason in *Gray v. Lewis*: the company never had control over the money in its bank account; it never could draw cheques upon it. Given the purpose served by share capital, such money could not constitute the company's share capital.

In these cases dishonest people used a circular transaction to inject fictitious money into a company in order to constitute its share capital. The critical payment was the payment to the company. The question was: was that an injection of share capital? Since the company could never have the use of the money, the answer was 'no'. Money received in such circumstances does not serve the purpose of share capital.

2 Buying a company's shares with its own money

Now let me turn to the cases where dishonest people use a circular transaction for the opposite purpose, to conceal the fact that they are extracting real money from the company by using it to fund the purchase of its own shares.

I will begin with another example from my own practice at the bar, this time when acting as a companies inspector. The owner of a controlling interest in a public company agreed to sell his shares for £150,000. Unfortunately, the purchaser did not have £150,000. So the parties organised a circular transaction in which the company itself would provide the purchase money. There were six players in the circle. The vendor and the purchaser made two; the company and a wholly owned subsidiary another two; and two newly formed offshore vehicle companies without any funds and operated by a complaisant accountant a further two.

The first step was for the vendor to borrow £150,000 from the company. The next step was for all six players to open a bank account at the same branch of a bank and to arrange a meeting with the branch manager. The plan was for the vendor to inject £150,000 into the circle by repaying his loan to the company; the company would pay the money to its subsidiary, which would pay it to one of the offshore companies, which would transfer it to the other, which would pay it to the purchaser, who would pay it to the vendor in payment for his shares. Unfortunately, the vendor did not have £150,000; he had only £25,000. This was no problem; he paid six cheques for £25,000 into the circle instead of a single cheque for £150,000, and the parties passed £25,000 round the circle six times. I was told that this procedure is known in the trade as 'tranching'.

It must have been a remarkable sight: Six men, sitting in a circle, each writing out six cheques for £25,000 and passing them to his neighbour who was busily doing the same; a total of thirty-six cheques each drawn on an account with nothing in it. This all took place under the watchful eye of the bank manager. What he thought was going on is not recorded; his only concern was to ensure that his bank did not give anyone any credit. Each of the six accounts had opening and closing balances of nil, but showed the receipt and payment of £150,000 during the day. The idea, of course, was to conceal the fact that the vendor's shares had been bought with the company's own money. It was assumed that no one would be able to investigate the two offshore companies and realise that the money movements were circular. It would appear that the company had received repayment of its loan and passed the money to its subsidiary to invest offshore. The source of the purchaser's funds would be hidden from view.

Now it is no use castigating the transaction as 'unreal' or a 'charade', or disregarding it because it was circular and without effect. It was all too effective. At the start of the operation the company had a debt due to it of £150,000; at the end it had been repaid and had parted with the proceeds but received nothing in return save an 'investment' in a worthless offshore company. It had lost £150,000.

The most celebrated instance of the use of circular money movements to purchase a company's shares with its own money is *Selangor United Rubber Estates Ltd v. Cradock (No. 3)*,[7] where there were two successive but independent circular transactions. The company was one of a number of cash shells that became targets for one Francis Cradock, the first defendant. He did not appear at the trial. By the time it began he was living in luxury on a yacht off Beirut and there were warrants out for his arrest in England.

Operating through a company called Woodstock, Cradock acquired a controlling shareholding in the company by the use of its own money by a circular transaction of the kind I have described. In consequence, Woodstock became liable to the company for a substantial sum. This was the first transaction. Later, by a second transaction, Woodstock sold its shareholding in the company to two men, Sinclair and Burden, and used the proceeds of sale to discharge its liability to the company. So far there was nothing improper in the transaction. But the payment was effected by the

---

7 [1968] 1 WLR 1555.

use of the company's money in the course of another circular movement of cheques. These were for identical sums which passed from Woodstock to the company in discharge of its liability to the company, from the company to Sinclair and Burden, and from Sinclair and Burden to Woodstock for the purchase of the company's shares. The only defendants worth suing were the company's banks and the company sued them for negligence. But the company had used different banks for the two transactions, so it was necessary to decide which transaction caused the loss. The bank that handled the first transaction argued that in the event it had caused the company no loss, since any loss had been made good by the second transaction.

Ungoed-Thomas J disagreed. He held that the loss was due to the first transaction, not the second. The second transaction caused no loss to the company because it failed to discharge Woodstock's liability in respect of the first transaction.

His Lordship held that the second transaction was not a sham or mere paper transaction. All the cheques were genuine and were intended to effect the payments for which they were tendered and they were all honoured. The critical payment was the payment by Woodstock to the company; and the question was whether it discharged Woodstock's liability to the company. The judge held that it was effective *as a payment* and that the absence of any underlying funds did not affect this conclusion.

But it did not follow that, because the payment was effective *as a payment*, it was effective to discharge Woodstock's liability, and his Lordship held that it was not. He said:[8]

> Such payments, if treated in isolation, would constitute satisfaction. But do they constitute satisfaction in the circumstances in which they were made? If these payments . . . were only made as part of the three cheque circular movements, *by which the payments to the [company] were dependent upon corresponding payments out by the [company's] directors from the [company's] account to the payer,* by a scheme in which the payer participates and without advantage to the [company], then the payer is giving with one hand what he at the same time takes away with the other. The [company] has the satisfaction of a conduit pipe. Even if one whistles half time when the money is in the [company's] hands, yet it must be the final result that matters in this as in other little games, the more so if the game is fraudulent and dishonest and fixed from the

8 ibid., 1651 (emphasis added).

> start. Satisfaction must be true and real satisfaction and not part of what makes satisfaction a mockery. I do not find it surprising that there is no authority for such a conclusion: and it is my conclusion.

In fact *Gray v. Lewis*, which was cited to Ungoed-Thomas J, is authority for his conclusion. In both cases the payment to the company was ineffective to achieve its purpose, in the one case to constitute the company's share capital and in the other to discharge the payer's liability to the company, in each case for the same reason; the company never obtained the use of the money.

Unfortunately, Ungoed-Thomas J also said that the company received no money capable of being misapplied; the second transaction merely substituted Burden and Sinclair's liability for Woodstock's; and as none of them was good for the money the transaction caused no loss.

Now this is something of a muddle. If the payment was effective *as a payment*, it must have been effective *as a receipt*; while if it was ineffective to discharge Woodstock's liability, it could not have substituted Burden and Sinclair's liability for Woodstock's. In *China Everbright-IHD Pacific Ltd v. Ch'ng Poh*,[9] the Court of

9 [2002] 5 HKCFAR 630.

Final Appeal of Hong Kong ventured to reformulate Ungoed-Thomas J's conclusion. We said that it was wrong to say that the company received no money capable of being misapplied. It was more accurate to say that it received no money which was not bound to be misapplied.

In *China Everbright*, there was only one transaction. The controlling shareholder agreed to sell his shares for HK$232 million. He and his associates owed the company $127 million. It was a term of the contract for the sale of the shares that on completion the vendor would deliver to the purchaser a banker's draft for HK$127 million in favour of the company in discharge of these loans.

Had the transaction been carried through normally, the purchaser would have paid $232 million to the vendor on completion and would have received bankers' drafts in favour of the company for $127 million for payment into the company's bank account. The purchaser, however, was unable to raise $232 million. Accordingly, he made arrangements to use the $127 million towards the payment of the purchase money due to the vendor on completion.

This was effected by a circular transaction, making use of bank cashier orders.

It was arranged that all the companies involved in the circulation of funds were customers of the same bank.

The first step was to appoint the purchaser to be chief executive of the company. The next step was to provide the bank with cheques for a total of $127 million drawn on the company's account in favour of its subsidiary Dixon, together with further cheques for the same total drawn on Dixon's account in favour of Wanfong, a nominee company owned by the bank.

On the morning of the day of completion Wanfong obtained cashier orders drawn on the bank's cashier order account in favour of the company for a total of $127 million. Wanfong authorised the bank to debit its account with the cost of the orders. There were at that stage no funds in its account, and the bank did not debit the account until later that same day.

Wanfong took the cashier orders to the completion meeting and handed them to the purchaser, who received them in his capacity as chief executive of the company. They were then taken back to the bank in order to be credited to the company's account.

Without the proceeds of the cashier orders there would have been insufficient funds in the company's account to transfer HK$127 million to Dixon; without the proceeds of the company's cheques in its favour there would have been insufficient funds in Dixon's account to support its cheques in favour of Wanfong; and without the proceeds of Dixon's cheques in its favour there would have been insufficient funds in Wanfong's account to pay for the cashier orders. But once the cashier orders had been returned to the bank the circle was complete, and the necessary entries were duly made in the various bank accounts. The value of the cashier orders, being $127 million, was credited to the company's bank account, and a like sum was immediately debited to the company's account, credited and debited to Dixon's account, credited to Wanfong's account, and finally debited to Wanfong's account in payment for the cashier orders. The paying-in slips were then taken to the completion meeting as evidence that the company had received the $127 million in discharge of the outstanding loans and that Wanfong (by the vendor's direction) had received the balance of the purchase price for the shares. The sale and purchase of the shares was then completed by the delivery of executed share transfers to the purchaser.

Thus the $127 million went round in a circle: from the bank (by means of cashier orders) to the company, from the company to its wholly owned subsidiary Dixon, from Dixon to the bank's vehicle company Wanfong, and from Wanfong (pursuant to the authority contained in its application for the cashier orders) back to the bank.

Since the money movements were circular, they did

not affect the cash position of any of the participants. Each of them paid out the identical sum that it received. But their net asset position was not unchanged. The payment of $127 million to the company was treated as discharging the outstanding loans; while the payment of $127 million by Dixon to Wanfong was treated as made in discharge of the purchase price for the shares in the company. It was beyond dispute that the purchaser used the company's funds to pay for shares in the company contrary to the provisions of the Companies Ordinance. Yet it was contended that the payment caused the company no loss.

The contention was, to say the least, counter-intuitive. Before the money movements the company had assets of $127 million, consisting of liabilities due to it; after the completion of the money movements those liabilities had been discharged and not replaced. The money paid to the company in discharge of liabilities due to it had been spent in acquiring shares in the company, but these belonged to the purchaser and not to the company. The value of the company's net assets had been reduced by $127 million. How could it be said that it had not suffered a loss of this amount?

The purchaser relied on the way in which Ungoed-Thomas J dealt with the second transaction in *Selangor*.

Just as the transaction did not discharge Woodstock's liability in that case, so (it was argued) it did not discharge the loans in the present case, with the result that the company suffered no loss. The trial judge and the Court of Appeal distinguished *Selangor* on the ground that the cashier orders were backed by real funds whereas the cheques in *Selangor* were not. This would draw a distinction between the case where the payments are made by the circulation of bankers' drafts or suitcases full of banknotes temporarily borrowed for the occasion and the case where they are discharged by ordinary cheques; yet the vice of the scheme does not lie in the absence of underlying funds but in the company's inability to make use of the money except for the purpose for which it is to be misapplied. Moreover, Ungoed-Thomas J had expressly held that the payments were effective as payments.

The factual position was indistinguishable from that in *Selangor*. But there was a crucial difference. In *Selangor* the company contended that the circulation of cheques did *not* discharge Woodstock's liability; so the question was whether it was *bound* to accept the payment as satisfaction when it could make no use of the money. In *China Everbright* the company contended that the circulation of cheques *did* discharge the indebtedness; so the question was whether the company was *entitled* to accept the payment as satisfaction. That is a different question. We held that it was.

If effective, the transaction would substitute one debtor for another. It is trite law that this cannot be done without the consent of the creditor. Because of the circular nature of the transaction, neither creditor had an opportunity to accept or reject the substitution at the time. In *Selangor* the company later rejected the substitution, with the result that it was ineffective for want of the company's consent. In *China Everbright* the company was content to accept the substitution, with the result that it was effective.

3 Tax avoidance

Let me now turn to the other category of case where circular money movements may be found: tax avoidance schemes. These raise much more difficult questions; they are not usually dishonest. The question is whether they achieve their object.

The leading case is, of course, *WT Ramsay Ltd v. Inland Revenue Commissioners*.[10] This concerned an artificial scheme in which not only the money movements but the transactions themselves were circular

---

10 [1979] 1 WLR 974.

and self-cancelling. They involved the creation of two assets of equal value, the transfer of value from one to the other, and the disposal of both for a total sum equal to their original cost. The disposal of one gave rise to an allowable loss and the disposal of the other to a corresponding gain which cancelled out the loss but was thought to be exempt from tax. At the end of the series of operations, the taxpayer's financial position was unchanged except for the payment of a fee to the promoter of the scheme. If the series of transactions was regarded as a whole, the taxpayer made neither a gain nor a loss. If each transaction in the series was regarded separately, however, they produced an allowable loss and a possibly exempt gain. The House of Lords held that they were to be regarded as a whole. Sir Anthony Mason has described the decision as involving both a rule of statutory construction and an approach to the analysis of the facts.[11]

The transactions recorded in the scheme documents in *Ramsay* were not shams. They were not intended to deceive. The documents were intended to have effect according to their tenor, and none of them was a cloak for any other transaction. If the documents concealed

[11] *Shiu Wing Ltd v. Commissioner of Estate Duty* [2000] 3 HKCFAR 215.

anything, it was that there was no underlying reality at all. They were an elaborate hocus-pocus; the transactions they purported to effect constituted nothing more than a financial round-robin, completely devoid of commercial reality, and achieving nothing beyond the obtaining of a tax deduction and payment of fees for the scheme. It was not merely that the various transactions had no motive except to obtain a tax advantage; they had no other purpose or effect. They were a complicated way of doing nothing. The lesson of the case is that you cannot obtain relief from tax by entering into a transaction that has no purpose or effect beyond the generation of relief from tax.

But it does not follow that circular transactions are incapable of generating tax consequences. In *MacNiven (HM Inspector of Taxes) v. Westmoreland Investments Ltd*[12] a circular movement of money was undertaken for the sole purpose of obtaining a tax advantage, but the House of Lords held that it was fiscally effective. A tax-exempt pension fund had a wholly owned subsidiary as a vehicle for its investments, using money lent to it by the fund. After a series of disastrous investments the company's liabilities greatly exceeded its assets, and it

12 [2003] 1 AC 311.

owed the fund some £70 million, including £40 million of accrued interest which it was unable to pay. Under the relevant statutory provisions, payments of interest may be set against profits and any unused excess carried forward to future years. If it paid the arrears of interest, therefore, the company would have a potential value to a purchaser as a company with established tax losses. But it had first to find the money to enable it to pay the interest. It had no resources of its own, so it borrowed the money from the fund.

This meant that the money went round in a circle. The company borrowed the money from the fund and repaid it to the fund in payment of the arrears of interest, deducting tax from the payment and accounting to the revenue for the tax. This had the effect of replacing its liability to pay interest with a liability for an equivalent capital sum and preserving the tax loss which would make it attractive to a purchaser. The fund (which was tax exempt) successfully reclaimed the tax that had been deducted and sold the company as a tax-loss company. The Commissioner, however, disallowed the subsequent claim by the company (now under new ownership) to set the interest payment against profits on the ground that the interest had not been 'paid' within the meaning of the tax code.

The Crown argued that a payment which comprises

a circular flow of money between borrower and lender and is made for no commercial purpose other than gaining a tax advantage does not constitute 'payment' within the meaning of the Taxing Acts. This was an attractive argument which at first sight appeared to be a straightforward application of *Ramsay*. But the House of Lords unanimously rejected it.

The tax advantage that the payment was designed to achieve was not the fund's ability to reclaim the tax that had been deducted. It was this feature that made the scheme unattractive to the Commissioner, but it was the consequence of the fund's tax-exempt status and this was not challenged. The object of the scheme was to preserve the company's right to charge interest payments against its profits, and it was this right that the Commissioner challenged. It was a right that predated the inception of the scheme but which the company would have lost if it could not obtain the money with which to pay the interest. Consideration of the purpose underlying the relevant statutory provisions showed that Parliament cannot have intended to draw a distinction between a payment made with money borrowed from a third party and money borrowed from the creditor. In this particular context, relief was not denied because the payment was made with a view to obtaining it.

The 'no business purpose test', therefore, is not

a free-standing principle that yields an automatic solution in every case. It is rather a manifestation of a purposive construction of the relevant statutory provisions, and even transactions undertaken for the sole purpose of obtaining relief from tax may be within the intendment of the statute.

Another scheme that employed circular money movements and that succeeded was *Shiu Wing Ltd v. Commissioner of Estate Duty*.[13] Mr Pong was a wealthy man who lived in Hong Kong and was worried at the imminent handover of the territory to China. He wished to protect his assets by placing them abroad, and to settle them on his children. These are both legitimate commercial purposes. He would still have wanted to place his assets abroad and settle them on his children even if estate duty did not exist.[14] But naturally he wished to avoid estate duty if he could. So he decided to take advantage of the rule that duty was not payable in respect of property situated outside Hong Kong. Had Mr Pong's assets consisted of money there would have been no difficulty. But they consisted of land in Hong Kong. So Mr Pong formed an overseas

---

13 [2000] 3 HKFCAR 215.

14 It has since been abolished in Hong Kong.

company, sold the land to the company, received the proceeds in Macau, and settled the proceeds of sale on an overseas trust for the benefit of his children.

The company had no money, so a series of circular payments was arranged. With the participants sitting in a bank in Macau, Mrs Pong borrowed money from the bank and lent it to the company, which used it to pay Mr Pong for the land; Mr Pong gave it to the trustees, who used it to subscribe for shares in the company, which used the money to repay Mrs Pong, who repaid the bank.

The Court of Appeal described the circular money movements as 'all smoke and mirrors', and held that the scheme fell foul of the *Ramsay* doctrine. The Court of Final Appeal reversed this decision and held that the scheme worked. This is surely right. The purpose of the scheme was to move Mr Pong's assets abroad before he settled them on his children. The critical transaction was the sale of the land. This converted Mr Pong's assets from land in Hong Kong to shares in an overseas company. The circular money movements were not of the essence. Mr Pong could have adopted a much simpler and more straightforward means to achieve his objective. He could simply have transferred the land to the company in exchange for shares in the company, and then given the shares to his children.

4 The film cases

Finally, I turn to two tax cases that involved the production of films. The schemes were of a kind that has been widely used, has excited the attention of the revenue authorities in many countries, and has frequently been challenged by them, sometimes successfully and sometimes not. The two cases I have chosen are paradoxical; the taxpayer who should have won, lost; and the taxpayer who should have lost, won.

The basic point about film production is that most films lose money; that is to say, they fail to generate sufficient net receipts after deducting the marketing and distribution costs to recoup the costs of production. The rewards of investing in a successful film, on the other hand, can be enormous. Studios make their money as distributors, and encourage investors to share the risks of actual production. To do so they may offer tax advantages.

The first case is *Ensign Tankers (Leasing) Ltd v. Stokes (Inspector of Taxes)*.[15] The taxpayer and others formed a limited partnership to produce a film called *Escape to Victory*. The film was to be made by a US studio and was to cost $13 million. The taxpayers were not willing

[15] [1992] 1 AC 655.

to put up more than 25 per cent of the cost, but their object was to obtain the benefit of 100 per cent of the first-year allowances in respect of the whole $13 million. They bought the film rights and screenplay and hired the director and actors, and commissioned the studio to make the film. The taxpayers would pay the cost of making the film as to 25 per cent out of their own money and as to 75 per cent out of money that they borrowed on a non-recourse loan from an associate of the studio, to be repaid only out of the net box office receipts. The studio remained in control of the money, debiting the loan account and crediting itself as it incurred the costs of making the film, thus giving rise to what looked suspiciously like circular money movements.

The Special Commissioners dismissed the taxpayers' appeal, holding that the transactions entered into by the taxpayers were not trading transactions. I allowed the appeal, and held that it was trading, and that *Ramsay* did not apply. The Court of Appeal allowed the Special Commissioners' appeal, holding that the transactions were not trading, and did not consider *Ramsay*. The House of Lords held that the transactions were trading transactions, but (as to 75 per cent) fell foul of *Ramsay*.

Lord Templeman held that the taxpayers had

incurred real expenditure of $3.25 million. Twenty-five per cent of the receipts were real receipts and generated a tax liability. The taxpayers were entitled to a first-year allowance equal to that expenditure. But the scheme had the 'apparently magic result'[16] of creating for tax purposes an expenditure of $13 million while incurring a real expenditure of only $3.25 million. The excess expenditure was not real expenditure. '[B]y reason of the non-recourse provision of the loan agreement the loan was not repayable by [the taxpayers] or any one else.'[17] He held that the true nature of the transaction was an investment by the taxpayers in return for a participation in profits. The accounting meant that 'the money . . . [was] at all times under the control of [the studio; and] was electronically transferred from Hollywood to the City of London and back again without serving any useful purpose and leaving no trace except entries on computer prints'.[18]

Lord Templeman was not saying that the money movements were circular. They were not. They passed from the lender in Hollywood to the investors in London and back to the production company in

---

16 ibid., 673.
17 ibid., 667.
18 ibid.

Hollywood, but there they were spent on making the film. They were not recirculated to the lender, whose debt remained outstanding and to be repaid out of the film receipts which would otherwise have been paid to the investors. Lord Templeman was saying that the insertion of the investors into the money movements served no purpose: the money could equally well have gone straight from the lender to the studio.

There are several difficulties with Lord Templeman's analysis. First, it does not explain why the lender was paying money to the studio, when there was no contract of loan between the lender and the studio; second, it does not reflect the commercial realities of the transaction; and, third, it assumes that, like most films, *Escape to Victory* would lose money.

First, the lender must be taken to have paid the money to the studio at the request of its borrowers, that is, the investors. So you cannot simply leave them out of account. Second, if the taxpayers had only a 25 per cent investment in the film, then the studio retained a 75 per cent interest, and could bring in other investors to share the risk (which it would obviously have liked to do). But the scheme made this impossible; the taxpayers owned the screenplay and film rights and had hired the director and actors. Moreover, the fact that the loan was a non-recourse loan did not mean that it did not have to be repaid; it did not have to be repaid by the taxpayers out of their own pockets, but it was repayable at their expense out of the film receipts. They needed to be brought into the money movements because they were the borrowers.

In fact, the film was highly successful; it made a lot of money; the non-recourse loan has long since been repaid; and the taxpayers have made large profits which, thanks to Lord Templeman, the Special Commissioners have been unable to tax.

The second case was *Peterson v. Commissioner of Inland Revenue*.[19] This was an outrageous scheme that deserved to fail but that succeeded. It involved the making of two films, one of which turned out to be a complete dud and was never released, and the other of which became the most successful film in New Zealand film history.

In each case the taxpayer was a member of a syndicate of investors that acquired the screenplay and the film and other rights and commissioned a film studio to produce the film for a fixed price. The film was expected to cost $x to make, but the investors were falsely led to believe that it would cost $x + y.

---

19 Unreported. Privy Council on appeal from New Zealand (Appeals Nos 66 of 2003 and 10 of 2004) (28 February 2005).

Accordingly, they were induced to sign a production contract by which they incurred a liability to pay \$x + y to the studio to make the film. This sum was payable in cash at the outset and was to be funded as to \$x by the investors out of their own resources and as to \$y by the proceeds of a non-recourse loan from a third-party lender connected with the studio. The investment was highly geared; \$y represented more than half (56.6 per cent) of the investors' total investment of \$x + y. The investors received \$y by way of a loan and paid it, together with \$x, out of their own resources to the studio in the discharge of their contractual liability. The studio applied \$x in making the film. Unknown to the investors, however, it did not use the \$y to make the film (for which it was not needed), but recycled the money to the lender immediately it was received.

The investors claimed to set off \$x + y against their taxable income as depreciation allowance. The Commissioner allowed \$x but disallowed \$y, which, it was said, was not part of the cost of making the film. This confused the cost to the investors, which was the relevant cost for the purposes of depreciation, and which was \$x + y, with the cost to the studio, which was only \$x, but which was irrelevant.

It is not surprising that the Commissioner challenged the scheme. The use of a non-recourse loan to leverage the amount of the investors' direct investment had the effect that they were not exposed to any risk of loss after tax relief was taken into account, so that in effect the films were being financed by the general body of taxpayers. The recycling of the loan demonstrated that it was not needed for and was not applied in film production. While there clearly was an underlying commercial activity with a potential for profit, the actual amount that was applied in that activity was only a small part of the investment for which tax relief was claimed. The underlying activity could not sustain the total amount of the investment that the investors claimed they had made.

But the Commissioner never got his act together. The Commissioner never pinpointed the critical payment, that is, the payment of $x + y to the production company, which was the payment for which depreciation allowance was claimed. He used a scatter-gun approach, and varied his aim as the case proceeded through the New Zealand courts. Before the Tax Court the Commissioner alleged that the scheme was a sham. This was rejected, and the Commissioner dropped the allegation. By the time the case reached the Court of Appeal the Commissioner was relying exclusively on the provisions of an anti-avoidance section, which allowed him to counteract a tax advantage in certain circumstances. As the Privy Council observed, this was a tacit admission that, but for the provisions of the statute, the scheme would have succeeded.[20]

The Court of Appeal thought that the obligation to repay $y out of the proceeds of the film was extinguished. This was because the money had passed back in a circle to the lender, thereby repaying the loan, which did not need to be repaid again from the proceeds of the film. The difficulty with this reasoning, which the Commissioner did not attempt to support before the Privy Council, is that they did not obtain a finding from the Tax Court, and there was no evidence that the studio paid the money to the lender in repayment of the loan. Moreover, it is impossible to reconcile it with the finding of the Tax Court that the investors knew nothing about the movement of the money (and therefore did not authorise the studio to repay the loan on their behalf) and the evidence that (in the case of the successful film) the investors have actually repaid the loan out of the film receipts.

The Court of Appeal did not decide the case on this ground, but held that the arrangement which could be counteracted under the section included the immediate

---

20 Otherwise there would be no tax advantage to counteract.

recycling of the loan to the lender so that 'the deduction for depreciation was overstated'[21] and the liability to pay $y was not 'truly incurred'.[22] This was a muddle. The recycling of the loan shows that the studio did not apply it to make the film; but it does not show that the investors did not pay it to the studio in order to acquire the film or incur a genuine liability to repay it out of the receipts of the film.

Before the Privy Council the Commissioner conceded that the investors incurred a contractual obligation to pay $x + y to the studio as the consideration for the making of the film; that they applied $y, the proceeds of the non-recourse loan, to the studio towards the performance of this obligation; and that the recycling of $y by the studio to the lender did not discharge the investors' liability to repay the loan out of the receipts of the film.

On these concessions the Privy Council (by a majority) allowed the taxpayer's appeal. But it observed that had the Commissioner obtained the necessary findings of fact from the Tax Court he might well have won.

---

21 *Peterson v. Commissioner of Inland Revenue*, unreported. Privy Council on appeal from New Zealand (Appeals Nos 66 of 2003 and 10 of 2004) (28 February 2005), para 24.

22 ibid.

The critical payment was the payment of \$x + y by the investors to the studio. This was the payment in respect of which depreciation allowance was claimed. In order to succeed, the Commissioner had to show that it was paid to acquire the film. The Commissioner never contended that the investors paid the money to the studio for any other purpose, so the choice was between holding that the money was not paid at all (i.e. that the payment was a sham, a finding which the Tax Court had rejected) or that it was paid to acquire the film.

But if the Tax Court had been asked to consider why the studio paid the \$y to the lender, which was never explained, it might have concluded that it paid the money in order to induce the lender to make the loan. Armed with such a finding, the Commissioner could plausibly have argued that the acquisition of the film was not the only consideration for which the investors paid the \$x + y to the studio; it was also paid in consideration for the studio's assistance in obtaining the loan. Where a single payment is made for two considerations, it may need to be apportioned. Here the apportionment would be straightforward; \$x was paid to acquire the film, which is a depreciable asset, and \$y to obtain the production company's assistance in obtaining the loan, which is not.

5 Conclusion

It is no good relying on rhetorical abuse and judicial indignation when faced with a circular transaction; and it is no good asking whether 'real money' was employed. It is necessary in every case to identify the critical payment, and ask whether it achieved its purpose; whether it be to provide a company with its share capital, or to discharge a liability owed to the company, or to obtain the benefit of a tax allowance.

There is no substitute for analysis.

THEFT OF IDENTITY

CHAPTER THREE

THEFT OF IDENTITY

Who am I? How am I to be identified? When I began my career more than fifty years ago, I was Peter Julian Millett of 18 Portman Close in the City of Westminster, Barrister-at-Law. That is how I asked my witnesses to identify themselves. 'What is your full name?' 'Where do you live?' 'What is your occupation?' My colleague Neuberger LJ tells me that he lost his first case with the second question he asked of his own client. He was appearing for a landlord who was seeking possession from a tenant of rent-controlled premises. In order to obtain possession, he had to show that he was living on the premises which he shared with the tenant. But when counsel asked, 'Where do you live?', his client gave a completely different address.

But who am I today? In most everyday transactions, whether on-line or by telephone or credit card, I increasingly identify myself by a PIN (Personal Identification Number), a user name (not the same as my ordinary name) or a password. Shops in England no longer accept payment by credit card accompanied by a signature; they require the customer's identity to be verified by a PIN. When I write a cheque, or give a direct debit instruction to my bank, I am asked to provide both my name and the number of my account. The banks were advised some years ago that the primary means of identification was the name of the account holder. But that advice is no longer consistent with practice. The banks' electronic systems are not programmed to recognise the name of the account holder. Although the banks still ask for both the name and the number of the relevant account, they ignore the name and rely exclusively on the account number. They have recently instructed William Blair QC, the Prime Minister's brother and our leading banking QC, to reconsider the previous advice and advise whether in future the banks can give primacy to the account number in law as well as in fact.

We are all becoming digitalised now. Of course, fraudulent impersonation has always been with us. But the growth in the number of credit transactions entered into electronically at a distance between persons unknown to each other, identifying themselves by PINs and passwords, coupled with the increasing electronic sophistication of the criminal fraternity, has led to a surge in what has been called 'theft of identity', that is, the fraudulent assumption by a rogue of another's identity in order to have the wrong account credited or debited or to misdirect enquiries into his own creditworthiness.

Take an everyday example. If I wanted cash in the old days, I went to the branch of my bank where I was well known and wrote out a cheque to cash. How antiquated! How inconvenient! But how fraud-proof! Today I go to an ATM (or 'hole-in-the-wall'), insert a debit card and type in a four-digit PIN. How convenient! But how open to fraud! The fraud is possible because the machine is programmed to supply cash to the person who produces the card and to debit the account of the person whose card is produced. The machine works on the assumption that the two are the same. But they may not be.

The scale of identity fraud in the United Kingdom is staggering. It has been estimated to cost the British economy some £1.7 billion a year. Thirteen thousand Jobcentre workers and one in seven employees of Network Rail had their identities stolen and used to obtain tax credits and welfare benefits. Of course, in these cases it is the government that has been defrauded, not the persons whose identities were taken. The greater use of PINs will not stop the frauds; only the introduction of bio-metric means of identification has any hope of doing that.

Fraudulent impersonation is a criminal offence. But I want to talk about the consequences for contractual liability. There is no problem in the example of the ATM. The bank will have unlawfully debited its customer's account without authority, and is liable to re-credit the account with the money wrongly taken from it. The account-holder may find it difficult to satisfy the bank that he did not use his card himself, but that is an evidential problem, not a legal one.

But false impersonation, or theft of identity, gives rise to a fundamental problem in the law of contract. A makes an offer to B. B accepts it, believing that he is dealing with C. A knows of B's mistake, and may have deliberately caused it. What is the result of the transaction? Is there a contract at all? There is obviously no contract with C, who is not a party to the transaction and knows nothing of it. But is there a contract with A? And, if so, is it void or merely voidable?

In the classic case, A, fraudulently masquerading as C, buys goods on credit from B; B, having conducted appropriate checks to satisfy himself that C is worthy of credit and believing A to be C, lets A have possession of the goods; and A thereupon sells the goods to D, an unsuspecting purchaser, before disappearing without paying for them. Who is to bear the loss? In the absence of legislation to the contrary, this depends on whether D, who has paid for the goods, has obtained title to them, for if D has not then B can reclaim them. But D will have obtained title only if A was able to transfer title to him, and this turns on whether the transaction between A and B resulted in a voidable contract for the purchase of the goods by A (which B will have been unable to avoid in time) or no contract at all.

The problem is occasionally mentioned in the contract textbooks in the section on offer and acceptance, but it is usually dealt with in the section on the effect of unilateral mistake, where it is said to turn on whether A's identity is sufficiently 'fundamental' to render the contract completely void. The fatal categorisation of the issue as one of unilateral mistake can be traced to Judah Benjamin,[1] was derived from Pothier and Savigny and the civil law, and was taken up by later writers on the law of contract. In his dissenting judgment in *Ingram v. Little*,[2] Devlin LJ distinguished between the

---

1 The author of *Benjamin on Sale*.

2 [1961] 1 QB 31, 64.

two questions and observed that it was easy to fall into error if one did not begin with the first question, whether there is sufficient correlation between offer and acceptance to bring a contract into existence at all. If there is, it is very difficult to justify holding the resulting contract to be altogether void rather than merely voidable.

The situation is seldom likely to arise in practice in the absence of fraud, and in the ordinary case where the fraud is not directed to the identity of the counterparty the contract is only voidable, not void, for the victim of deception ought to be free to elect to affirm the contract if he chooses to do so. It is difficult to see why a mistake induced by fraud should make a contract altogether void if it is a mistake as to the identity of the counterparty and not if it is a mistake as to some other material attribute of his such as his creditworthiness. After all, in a credit transaction A's identity as such is immaterial; it is merely the key to enable B to run a credit check: the attribute that induces acceptance of A's offer is his supposed creditworthiness, not his identity.

As between A and B themselves, of course, it does not normally matter whether the contract is void or merely voidable; it obviously cannot be enforced by A against B's wishes in either case. The question usually assumes importance only where an innocent third party is involved, and then it is critical. Under the law as it stands in England at present, his title depends on whether A obtained the goods in his own name by means of a false or forged credit reference, or by masquerading as C and using a genuine reference relating to C. This is surely indefensible. The law should surely favour a solution that protects innocent third parties by treating the contract as voidable rather than void, whether for fraud or for mistake.

More than thirty years ago[3] Lord Denning MR roundly rejected the theory that if a party is mistaken as to the identity of the person with whom he is contracting there is no contract, or that if there is a contract it is null and void so that no property can pass under it. He said that the doctrine, derived from the writings of Pothier, should not be admitted as part of English law but should be 'dead and buried' altogether.

Three years ago the House of Lords had the opportunity to follow Lord Denning's lead, but it did not take it. In *Shogun Finance Ltd v. Hudson*,[4] by a majority of three to two, it affirmed the traditional view that there was no contract and the innocent purchaser obtained no title. Lord Nicholls and I dissented.

A fraudulent rogue (A) visited a car showroom and

---

3 *Lewis v. Averay* [1972] 1 QB 198, 206–207.

4 [2004] 1 AC 919.

offered to buy a car on hire-purchase. He produced a stolen driver's licence in C's name, and filled in the hire-purchase form with C's name and address and signed it in C's name. The dealer telephoned the details through to his finance company, who ran a credit check on C. The results proved satisfactory; the dealer signed the hire-purchase form as agent for the finance company, took a worthless cheque for the deposit, and let A drive the car away. A few days later A sold the car to D. The cheque bounced; the finance company traced the car, and demanded possession from D. D claimed that he had bought it in good faith and was the owner. He lost.

No one would doubt the correctness of this result at common law. A's use of C's name would be immaterial. He had only bought the car on hire-purchase; he did not own the car but had only hired it; and he had no title to pass to D. But such frauds, not involving theft of identity, where a person buys a car on hire-purchase and sells it to an unsuspecting purchaser, had become very common in England, and Parliament had intervened by enacting legislation to provide that, where a hirer under a hire-purchase agreement sold the car to a bona fide purchaser, the purchaser should obtain a good title. So the question for the House of Lords was: was there a valid contract of hire-purchase between the finance company and A?

Simple notions of justice surely demand an affirmative answer. Why should the innocent purchaser keep the car if his vendor had obtained it by forging a credit reference in his own name but lose it if his vendor had obtained it by masquerading as someone else? Surely the precise mechanics of the fraud should not affect D, who has no means of enquiry. It is a classic case where the question is which of two innocent people should suffer loss as a result of the fraud of a third party. As between the finance company and D, there is much to be said for making the finance company suffer the loss. It could easily have prevented the fraud by contacting C, whose name and address had been provided, and asking him to confirm that he wished to proceed with the transaction. Had the case come within certain statutory provisions, the finance company would have been obliged to do this, not as a protection against fraud, but in order to give C a 'cooling-off period'.

In the absence of further legislation, the question is now settled in England in favour of B (the finance company). It is also settled but in favour of D in the United States, where the Uniform Commercial Code provides:[5]

---

5 Article 2-403(1) (14th edn, 1995).

> A person with voidable title has power to transfer a good title to a good faith purchaser for value. When goods have been delivered under a transaction of purchase the purchaser has such power even though
> (a) the transferor was deceived as to the identity of the purchaser.[6]

I believe that the question is not settled in Australia. So I hope that it will be a useful exercise to explore the legal position in more detail.

The majority of my colleagues in *Shogun* were unwilling to depart from the celebrated decision of the House of Lords in *Cundy v. Lindsay*,[7] a decision that had stood unchallenged for more than 120 years. It is a case that is familiar to every law student in England and, I imagine, in Australia too. I found it an extraordinary experience to find myself sitting in the House of Lords and considering the correctness of a decision of the House that I had come

---

6 Under German law, too, the innocent third party obtains a good title, though this is a consequence of the law of property rather than the law of contract. Article 932 of the German Civil Code provides that a purchaser acting in good faith acquires title where he obtains possession from a seller who has no title. The purchaser is not in good faith if he knew, or by reason of gross negligence did not know, that the goods did not belong to the seller.

7 (1878) 3 App Cas 459.

across in my first year as a law student some fifty years earlier.

A rogue named Blenkarn, posing as Blenkiron & Co., ordered goods by letter from the plaintiffs. They replied to the letter, accepted the order and despatched the goods to the name and address given in the letter. Blenkarn then sold them to the defendants. The House of Lords held that the defendants obtained no title.

Unlike most fraudsters, Blenkarn did not simply disappear. He was arrested and convicted of obtaining property by false pretences. The House of Lords held that the conviction necessarily meant that the contract for sale was void. If their Lordships had stopped there, the case could be put on one side as obsolete. Unfortunately, they did not; they went on to consider the contractual position, and held that no contract ever came into existence between Blenkarn and the plaintiff.

It did not take long for the case to be regarded as holding that a mistake as to the identity of the counterparty, unlike any other mistake, meant that any apparent contract was void. Both Pollock and Anson's treatises on the law of contract cited the case for this proposition. Indeed, Anson considered that fraudulent impersonation was an exception to the general rule that a contract procured by fraud was voidable at the option of the defrauded party. Pollock and Anson established unilateral mistake as to identity as a distinct category in the law of contract.

But this was not the basis of the decision. The word 'mistake' appears only once in the five speeches, and then only in reference to the address of the premises to which the plaintiffs had despatched the goods. Lord Cairns LC observed that it was not a case in which a contract could be impeached for fraud, but where a contract never came into existence at all. There was no contract between the plaintiffs and the cheat Blenkarn because:

> [o]f him they knew nothing, and of him they never thought. With him they never intended to deal. Their minds never, even for an instant of time, rested upon him, and as between him and them there was no *consensus* of minds which could lead to any agreement or contract whatever. As between him and them there was merely the one side to a contract where, in order to produce a contract, two sides would be required.[8]

Lord Hatherley spoke to the same effect:

---

[8] ibid., 465–66.

> . . . if there could be said to have been any sale at all, it failed for want of a purchaser.[9]

It was not a sale to Blenkarn,

> with whom the [plaintiffs] had not, and with whom they did not wish to have, any dealings whatever.[10]

The defendants (D) lost because there was no contract of sale between their vendor (the rogue) (A) and the plaintiffs (B). There was clearly a transaction between them, for B had delivered possession of the goods to A with the intention that he should be free to deal with them as owner. But there was no contract of sale and purchase. It is trite law, as Devlin LJ explained in *Ingram v. Little*,[11] that before a contract can come into existence there must be offer and acceptance, and these must correspond. The offer must be addressed to the offeree, either as an individual or as a member of a class or of the public. The acceptance must come from one who is so addressed and must itself be addressed to the offeror. It is not possible in law for a person to

---

9 ibid., 467.
10 ibid.
11 [1961] 1 QB 31.

accept an offer made to someone else, or to intercept an acceptance of someone else's offer and treat it as an acceptance of his own.

But as Professor Treitel has observed,[12] a person may be identified by reference to any of his attributes. He may be identified as 'the person in the room', 'the person who spoke on the telephone', 'the person who appended the illegible signature', 'the writer of the letter under reply' or 'the person who made the offer'; but he may also be identified as 'the person whose creditworthiness has been checked and found to be satisfactory'. Any of these may be the means of identifying a unique person.

As an authority on the formation of contract, *Cundy v. Lindsay* is, with respect, unconvincing. Why should the counterparty not be identified as 'the writer of the letter under reply'? That the plaintiffs did not wish to have any dealings with Blenkarn is beyond dispute; but it is far from obvious that they did not actually have such a dealing, even though it was only as a result of the deception practised on them. Lord Cairns dwelt on the plaintiffs' subjective state of mind, which was of course affected by the fraud, and gave no attention to

---

12 GH Treitel, *The Law of Contract*, 11th edn, Thomson Sweet & Maxwell, London, 2003, pp. 298–99.

the question whether, approaching the case objectively, they had accepted Blenkarn's offer. Lord Penzance[13] initiated the unfortunate distinction between cases of persons dealing in the presence of each other and other cases, without explaining why this was material, let alone decisive.

The plaintiffs, indeed, 'knew nothing' of the individual named 'Blenkarn' and they addressed their letter of acceptance to 'Blenkiron & Co.'. But that is because they had been deceived into believing that the offer came from Blenkiron & Co. Throughout the speeches in the House it was assumed that the plaintiffs' letter of acceptance was directed and sent, as the goods were later directed and sent, to the intended recipient (Blenkiron & Co.) but at the wrong address. If the facts are considered objectively, however, with a view to ascertaining whether there was the necessary correlation between offer and acceptance and without reference to the deception, the matter wears a very different aspect. The order was placed by Blenkarn (posing as Blenkiron & Co.) writing from his own address (which was not the address of Blenkiron & Co.) and was duly accepted by the plaintiffs in the belief that

13 (1878) 3 App Cas 459, 471–72.

the order came from Blenkiron & Co. They replied to Blenkarn (in his assumed name as Blenkiron & Co.) at the address he had given (being his own address and not that of Blenkiron & Co.) by a letter that referred to and accepted his order; and in due course they fulfilled it.

I consider that the proper conclusion on these facts is that the plaintiffs contracted with Blenkarn in the mistaken belief, induced by his fraud, that they were dealing with Blenkiron & Co., and that the resulting contract was voidable for fraud. If the plaintiffs' subjective state of mind, induced by the fraud, is put to one side, there is no justification for the question-begging assumption that their letter of acceptance was directed to Blenkiron & Co. and that it was the name that was right and the address that was wrong. Looked at objectively, the plaintiffs' letter was manifestly intended to be an acceptance of the offer contained in the letter under reply.

Ever since *Cundy v. Lindsay*, judges have tried to limit its effect by adopting Lord Penzance's suggestion and distinguishing between transactions entered into at a distance (e.g. by correspondence) and transactions entered into orally between parties who are in the presence of each other. In the former case, B's intention is ascertained by construing the description of the counterparty in the contract. This naturally identifies C, the person whose identity A has fraudulently assumed, and (provided that C actually exists) inevitably leads to the conclusion that there is no counterparty and therefore no contract. In the latter case, the courts have introduced a rebuttable presumption that, where parties deal with each other face to face, each of them intends to contract with the physical person to whom he addresses the words of contract. Unless the presumption is rebutted, this must lead to the conclusion that there is a contract with the impostor.

Phillips v. Brooks[14] was a case where the sale was over the counter. A came into B's shop and bought an expensive ring on credit by pretending to be Sir George Bullough, a well-known and wealthy local resident. Horridge J distinguished *Cundy v. Lindsay* and held that the rogue obtained a good title which he had passed to D. He ruled that the shopkeeper had:

> contracted to sell and deliver [the ring] to the person who came into his shop . . . who obtained the sale and delivery by means of the false pretence that he was Sir George Bullough . . . [The shopkeeper's] intention was to sell to the person present and identified by sight and hearing.[15]

---

[14] [1919] 2 KB 243.

[15] ibid., 246–47.

Horridge J treated the identity of the purchaser as a question of fact to be determined objectively and without regard to the evidence that the shopkeeper had no intention of selling the goods to anyone other than Sir George Bullough.

That is surely correct. But why should D's title depend on whether his vendor bought the goods by a face-to-face transaction or by correspondence?

Another artificial distinction was drawn in *King's Norton Metal Co. Ltd v. Edridge Merrett & Co. Ltd.*[16] In that case the contract was entered into by correspondence, but the rogue (Wallis) assumed a fictitious name (Hallam & Co.) in order to give a spurious impression of respectability. The Court of Appeal held that there was a valid (though voidable) contract. The decisive feature was that there was no one of the assumed name. AL Smith LJ is reported as having argued as follows:[17]

> The question was, 'With whom, upon this evidence, which was all one way, did the plaintiffs contract to sell the goods?' *Clearly with the writer of the letters.* If it could have been shown that there was a separate entity called

[16] (1897–98) 14 TLR 98.

[17] ibid., 99 (emphasis added).

> Hallam and Co. and another entity called Wallis then the case might have come within the decision in 'Cundy v. Lindsay'. In his opinion there was a contract by the plaintiffs with the person who wrote the letters, by which the property passed to him. There was only one entity, trading it might be under an *alias*, and there was a contract by which the property passed to him.

But why on earth should D's title depend on whether A used the name of a real or a fictitious person? A possible explanation of *King's Norton Metal Co. Ltd v. Edridge Merrett & Co. Ltd* is that A merely assumed a false name and did not go further and assume another person's identity. But the distinction is a fine one, if it exists at all. In any case, it depends on the nature and mechanics of the deception and while relevant to its effect on the mind of the offeree ought not to be relevant to the correlation between offer and acceptance. If B contracted with the writer of the letters under reply in *King's Norton Metal*, why did B not contract with the writer of the letter in *Cundy v. Lindsay*?

The introduction of a rebuttable presumption of fact in this context is unhelpful, since it is unclear what evidence is sufficient to rebut the presumption. As Devlin LJ stressed, it cannot be rebutted by piling up evidence that B would never have accepted the offer if he had not thought that it had been made by C. Such evidence merely shows that the deception was material; it does not establish the identity of B's counterparty. There is surely nothing to be said for resorting to a rebuttable presumption in order to resolve a question of fact that is incapable of being determined by evidence. If there is no test by which the question can be answered on the evidence, there is none by which the court can determine whether the presumption has been rebutted.

In *Ingram v. Little*, Pearce LJ said: 'Each case must be decided on its own facts.'[18] This is singularly unhelpful, since it involves asking: did B intend to contract with A believing him to be C? or with C believing him to be A? The question is meaningless. As Devlin LJ pointed out in the same case:[19]

> If Miss Ingram had been asked whether she intended to contract with the man in the room or with P. G. M. Hutchinson, the question could have no meaning for her, since she believed them to be one and the same. The reasonable man of the law – if he stood in Miss Ingram's shoes – could not give any better answer . . . All that Miss Ingram or any other witness in her position can say

---

18 [1961] 1 QB 31, 61.
19 ibid., 65 (emphasis added).

> is *that she did in fact accept the offer made to her;* and that, if she had not been tricked or deceived, she would not have accepted it.

In fact, the distinction between face-to-face transactions and transactions at a distance is unsound. If the offeree's words of acceptance are taken to be addressed to the physical person standing in his presence who made the offer, why is the same not true of the contract entered into by correspondence? Why is an offeree's letter of acceptance not taken to be addressed to the physical person whose written offer is under reply? The offeree addresses the offeror by his assumed name in both cases. Why should this be disregarded in the one case and yet treated as decisive in the other? Indeed, the correlation between offer and acceptance is likely to be greater in the case of a contract entered into by correspondence, since the offeree's letter of acceptance will either be sent to the impostor at his own address or be delivered to him personally and it will almost certainly contain internal references to his offer. Moreover, if the offeree's words of acceptance are taken to be addressed to the physical person standing in his presence who made the offer, what is the position where they deal with each other by telephone? Is the disembodied voice to be equated with physical presence?

Is it sufficient that the parties are in the hearing of each other? Does it make a difference if they deal with each other by televisual link, so that the parties are in the hearing and sight but not the presence of each other? New means of communication make the distinction untenable.

As an authority on the formation of contract, *Cundy v. Lindsay* is vitiated by its subjective approach; and textbook writers usually treat it as an example of unilateral mistake even though this was not the basis on which it was decided. It has had a baleful influence on the development of the law, leading to an unprincipled distinction between face-to-face transactions and others and the indefensible conclusion that an innocent purchaser's position should depend on the nature of the mistake of a third party or the precise mechanics of a fraud perpetrated on him. My colleagues in the House of Lords were unwilling to depart from a decision of the House that had stood for more than 120 years, even though it had been followed reluctantly by courts that were bound by it and distinguished wherever possible. I hope that the High Court of Australia may be bolder.

If there is legislation in England, it is likely to follow the model of the US Uniform Commercial Code by carving out a further exception to the *nemo dat quod non habet* rule rather than by changing the rules of offer and acceptance. So it may be useful to consider a trio of cases where D was not present and the issue was raised squarely between A and B.

The first is the famous case of *Said v. Butt.*[20] The plaintiff was a theatre critic who wished to attend the first night of a play. He had had serious differences of opinion with the management of the theatre, and he knew that an application for a ticket in his own name would be refused. So he arranged for a friend to go to the theatre and buy a ticket for him. When he turned up for the performance he was refused admission. His claim for damages was dismissed. The evidence showed that a first night is a special event with characteristics of its own, and that first-night tickets are only given or sold to persons whom the management selects and wishes to favour. McCardie J found that the purchaser's identity was a material element in the formation of the contract and that the purchaser's failure to disclose the fact that he was buying the ticket on the plaintiff's behalf prevented the plaintiff from taking up the ticket. In my opinion that conclusion is inescapable. The case is usually taken to be an example of a contract that is

[20] [1920] 3 KB 497.

void for mistake. I do not think that it is. There can be no doubt that the friend who bought the ticket could have made use of it to gain admission for himself. In my opinion, the case has nothing to do with mistake, or fraud, or even offer and acceptance. It is an application of the principle that an undisclosed principal cannot intervene where the nature of the contract shows that it was intended to be with the agent personally.[21] The evidence showed that first-night tickets are not transferable, from which it follows that they are incapable of being bought for an undisclosed principal, so that on its own terms the contract could not be enforced by the plaintiff.

The second case is *Hector v. Lyons*.[22] It is a very curious case. It concerned a contract for the sale and purchase of land. Mr Hector Senior negotiated with Mrs Lyons for the purchase of her property. They negotiated personally, at first over the telephone and then face to face. Throughout the negotiations, for a reason that was never explained, Mr Hector Senior used the name of his son, Mr Hector Junior, who was under-age. It is not clear whether the parties entered into an

---

21 See *Collins v. Associated Greyhound Racecourses Ltd* [1930] 1 Ch 1 (CA).

22 (1989) 58 P & CR 156.

agreement subject to contract, but if they did it would have been signed by Mr Hector Senior in his son's name. He instructed solicitors to act for him, again in his son's name, and in due course contracts were signed and exchanged, the two parts being in identical terms and giving Mr Hector Junior's name as the name of the purchaser. Mr Hector Senior signed his part of the contract in his son's name. Mrs Lyons refused to complete and Mr Hector Senior brought an action for specific performance. He did so in his own name. Sir Nicolas Browne-Wilkinson V-C dismissed the action.

It has been suggested that the action rightly failed because there was no identity between the name of the plaintiff in the writ and that in the contract which he was claiming to enforce. But this was not the ground of decision and is without substance. The objection could readily be met if necessary by amending the writ to add after the name of the plaintiff the words 'also known as . . .'

It might have been an understandable ground for refusing equitable relief that it was not at all clear to the Court what was going on,[23] particularly as Mr Hector Senior's testimony was thoroughly unsatisfactory.

---

[23] I suspect that it was an amateurish attempt at estate duty evasion.

But that was not the basis of the decision either. The Vice-Chancellor held that there was no contract. The identity of the parties to a written contract was established, as a matter of construction, by the names stated in the contract. The only question for the Court was to identify who they were, and this was a question of fact.

It was certainly established that the *name* of the purchaser stated in the contract was the name of Mr Hector Junior and not that of Mr Hector Senior. But it does not at all follow that *the party who contracted as purchaser in that name* was Mr Hector Junior. The evidence plainly showed that it was not. He knew nothing of the transaction, and Mrs Lyons did not deal or intend to deal with him. To adapt Lord Cairns's words in *Cundy v. Lindsay* (but in the converse case, for we are now talking of C, not of A), 'of him she knew nothing, and of him she never thought. With him she never intended to deal.'[24]

I think the evidence demonstrated beyond doubt that the purchaser was in fact Mr Hector Senior, who for some reason of his own had adopted his son's name for the purpose of entering into the contract. He was identified as the person who in fact negotiated the

---

24 (1878) 3 App Cas 459, 465–66.

purchase with Mrs Lyons and agreed to pay the purchase price, who signed any agreement subject to contract that there may have been, who instructed solicitors to act on his behalf as purchaser, and who signed the purchaser's part of the contract. Mrs Lyons was neither deceived nor mistaken. She not only intended to deal but actually dealt with Mr Hector Senior. The only fact in respect of which she was mistaken was that the name in which he contracted was not his real name but that of his son, and that was not material. If the Court was concerned that there was some trickery involved, it could have ordered the conveyance to be taken in Mr Hector Senior's name.

The Vice-Chancellor held that the identification of the parties to a written instrument is a question of construction. That is certainly the first step in the process, and usually it will be enough. But once it is established that the person whose name and other personal details are stated in the contract and the person who stated them and signed the contract are not the same, the question immediately arises: which of them should be treated as the counterparty? Do the name and other details included in the contract refer to the person to whom they belong or to the impostor who included them in order to identify himself? This is not simply a question of construction. It is partly a question of fact and partly a question of law. To say, as Lord Hobhouse did in *Shogun*, that it is a question of construction which admits of only one answer, simply begs the question.

The last case is the old case of *Boulton v. Jones*,[25] which was decided before *Cundy v. Lindsay* and can usefully be contrasted with it. It is the only case in the series in which there was no deceit. It is about offer and acceptance, and nothing else. The defendant sent to the shop owned by one Brocklehurst a written order for goods. The order was addressed to Brocklehurst by name. Unknown to the defendant, Brocklehurst had earlier that day sold and transferred his business to Boulton. Boulton executed the order and delivered the goods to the defendant without notifying him that he had taken over the business. The defendant accepted the goods and consumed them in the belief that they had been supplied by Brocklehurst. When he received Boulton's invoice he refused to pay it, claiming that he had intended to deal with Brocklehurst personally, since he had dealt with him previously and had a set-off on which he had intended to rely. The Court of Exchequer held that the defendant was not liable for the price.

---

[25] (1857) 2 H & N 564.

There was a preliminary question of construction, whether the defendant's order could be construed as addressed not to Brocklehurst personally but to the proprietor of the shop for the time being. The Court held that it could not. This point need not detain us further.

Three of the four judges decided the case on the straightforward ground that the offer was addressed to Brocklehurst and could not be accepted by Boulton.[26] Looked at objectively, there was no correlation between offer and acceptance. This is the same ground as that which later formed the basis of the decision in *Cundy v. Lindsay*, but the facts of the two cases are very different. In *Boulton v. Jones* the goods were ordered from Brocklehurst but supplied and invoiced by Boulton; the acceptance did not correspond with the offer. In *Cundy v. Lindsay* the goods were ordered by Blenkarn posing as Blenkiron & Co. and supplied and invoiced to him in that name. Outwardly the acceptance did correspond with the offer. Objectively speaking there was *consensus ad idem,* though this was vitiated by the fraud that produced it.

---

26 It is best to disregard the judgment of Bramwell B, which, though the most frequently cited, was condemned by Dr Goodhart as the least satisfactory.

The case has a point of further interest to lawyers today. Why was the defendant not liable for the price? He was not contractually liable, since there was no contract of purchase. But he had received the goods and consumed them; why was he not liable on a *quantum valebat*?

In 1857 *quantum meruit* and *quantum valebat* claims were regarded as claims in contract, arising from an implied promise to pay for goods supplied or services rendered. But it was a condition of liability that the goods or services should have been obtained in circumstances from which a promise to pay for them could be implied. In this case, however, it was not possible to imply a promise on the part of the defendant to pay for the goods in the face of evidence that he never intended to pay for the goods but to rely on his set-off.

We would analyse it differently today. Claims in *quantum meruit* and *quantum valebat* are no longer regarded as contractual or as depending on an implied promise to pay. They are claims in restitution. The law imposes an obligation to pay for goods supplied or services rendered in order to prevent unjust enrichment. The defendant must return the goods or pay for them. This would today be the basis of the defendant's liability; but he would have a good defence – the defence of innocent change of position. He had consumed the goods in the genuine and reasonable belief that he did *not* have to pay for them.

I regard the case as an early example of the change-of-position defence succeeding almost 140 years before the principle was accepted into English law.

INDEX